UNREAL ESTATE

Robert de Gast

UNREAL ESTATE

The Eastern Shore

THE JOHNS HOPKINS UNIVERSITY PRESS   BALTIMORE AND LONDON

The Johns Hopkins University Press

2715 North Charles Street

Baltimore, Maryland 21218-4319

The Johns Hopkins Press Ltd., London

LIBRARY OF CONGRESS CATALOGING-IN-PUBLICATION DATA

De Gast, Robert, 1936–

    Unreal estate : the Eastern Shore / by Robert de Gast.

       p.   cm.

    ISBN 0-8018-4412-6.—ISBN 0-8018-4591-2 (pbk.)

    1. Eastern Shore (Md. and Va.)—Pictorial works. I. Title.

F232.E2D4 1993

779'.997521—dc20   91-47048

FOR EVELYN, AGAIN

The true basis for any serious study of the art of Architecture still lies in those indigenous, more humble buildings everywhere that are to architecture what folklore is to literature or folk song to music.

FRANK LLOYD WRIGHT
The Sovereignty of the Individual, 1910

PREFACE

My interest in abandoned structures began about ten years ago, when, for nearly five thousand dollars, I bought a lot on the main street of the charming village of Harborton, on the Chesapeake Bay side of the Eastern Shore of Virginia. There was, to be sure, a small house on the lot, but it had been unoccupied for several years and seemed unsalvageable; it was assumed by the seller (and the neighbors) that the house was to be torn down, and perhaps a new one built. Things looked hopeless. My father, who had survived two wars in Europe, refused to go inside when I proudly showed him my new acquisition. It looked, he said, like it had been bombed, and it certainly didn't look very safe.

But in fact it was safe. The structure was basically sound. It had been built with care and sound materials. I thought I could salvage it. Certainly the task seemed daunting: windows were broken; doors were off their hinges; trash was everywhere; the floors and walls signaled decades of neglect. There was no running water and no electricity. But, after nearly one hundred years, the house was free of termites and rot and once even had been pretty. An entire summer and part of fall was spent restoring and updating the house. A year later I had the pleasure of having an architect tell me that this tiny house contained some of the finest human-sized spaces he had ever experienced.

For nearly five years it was a comfortable and cozy residence for my wife and me. Having saved the dwelling from the wrecker's ball was a particularly satisfying experience. It is not something I would recommend for everyone, but it solidified my interest in abandoned buildings of all kinds, and in their place in the American landscape.

The Eastern Shore of Virginia is a peculiar fraction of that landscape—a narrow peninsula, bounded on the east by the Atlantic Ocean and on the west by the Chesapeake Bay. Fifty years ago, the *WPA Guide to Virginia* described the peninsula this way:

US 13 drops down the middle of Virginia's Eastern Shore on a fairly straight course to Cape Charles near the tip of the narrowed peninsula that separates Chesapeake Bay from the ocean. The fertile land of Accomack County—the northern two-thirds of this peninsula—is abundantly wooded and rolls gently out to marshy flats along both coasts, which are interlaced by innumerable inlets and shallow bays. A chain of low islands along the east protects the mainland from the full force of Atlantic storms. These sheltered waters abound with fish and shellfish, which form one of the chief sources of local income. Most of Northampton County, the other third of the peninsula, is absolutely flat.

Truck farms dotted with neatly-kept white frame houses stretch away to the dark green walls of pine woods, which form windbreaks against wintry gales. This landscape makes a curious impression; it is as though everything in sight has been laid out with T-square and compass. At the end of long side roads, houses, occasionally of brick and very old, stand in solitude on meadowy lawns close to the water.

Little of the natural delight of the place has changed since the 1930s, but first-time visitors to the Shore (always capitalized) now invariably comment on the number of abandoned buildings. There are, of course, abandoned buildings to be found anywhere, but not, I think, in the same astonishing profusion as on the Shore. There are many abandoned buildings in parts of the Carolinas, in the desert Southwest, and in portions of the Midwest, but the small size of Virginia's Eastern Shore—its 682 square miles amount to less than $1/_{60}$ of the area of the Commonwealth of Virginia, and a population of fewer than 50,000 gives it less than $1/_{500}$ of the state's residents—emphasizes the number of derelict structures.

The Shore is criss-crossed by almost a thousand miles of state-maintained roads, and it would be difficult to find a mile stretch without an abandoned store, church, gas station, lifesaving station, lookout tower, or (most often) a house. The abandoned ruins are located near villages, towns, and crossroads with intriguing names like Mutton Hunk, Frogstool, Cats Bridge, and Birdsnest; with names reflecting the livelihood of the inhabitants, like Clam and Oyster; and with names showing interesting moral and financial issues, like Temperanceville and Modest Town, or Cashville, Pennyville, Cheapside, and Greenbackville. Other names are reminders of the Shore's first inhabitants: Pungoteague, Chincoteague, Kiptopeke, and Assawoman.

Buildings, especially homes, are usually abandoned as a result of both declining population and depressing circumstances. Accomack and Northampton counties have had much of both. From a high of 53,000 in 1910, the Shore population lost ten thousand over the following sixty years. Depression in the 1930s accounted for much of the drop, as did the exodus of people to Norfolk, Newport News, Baltimore, and other cities for work during World War II. During the war, and especially afterward, mechanization led to larger farms—and the need for fewer laborers. The trend has continued, and of late the demand for farm laborers on the Shore at harvest times has been met by Mexican migrant workers. Today the counties of Accomack and Northampton are among the poorest in the state. Median income in Virginia is around $30,000, but on the Eastern Shore it remains at less than $17,000.

The untold number of abandoned buildings is therefore a constant reminder of the poverty and depression in these two counties, a continual sign of failure. For, as romantic as abandoned structures may appear, each abandonment signals a failed dream, or a bankrupted business, or family sadness. As David Lowenthal wrote in *The Past Is a Foreign Country*, "Tumble-down houses are distressing because they betoken failure to forestall decay. The keenest admirers of decay admit that beyond a point it no longer beautifies." Lowenthal went on to note that different people have different views as to when that point has arrived.

Strange as it sounds, Ada Louise Huxtable was probably right when she said, "There is no art as impermanent as architecture." Impermanence is obviously more of a truth when the buildings, as they are almost always on the Shore, are built of wood. Wooden buildings can and do survive for a long time, but only if the greatest of care is lavished on them. And so a mansion may survive, while the slave quarters perish. (Mobile homes, a more recent attempt to provide inexpensive housing, do not last nearly as long as well-built wood frame houses, and so are abandoned more quickly, although their final decay will take infinitely longer.) The 1980 census listed 19,947 dwellings, including mobile homes, on the Eastern Shore of Virginia, of which 7,653 were built before World War II. The count for single-family houses was down nearly one thousand since the previous census in 1970. Most of these were abandoned, although some were destroyed by fire or were demolished.

The abandonment of houses is often gradual: a home may be vacated by a tenant farmer, then used as temporary migrant housing, and finally used as a storage depot for seed or fertilizer. There are no laws requiring the demolition of abandoned buildings, and many people would resent them. Proud of their independence, they don't like any one telling them what to do about their private property. "Besides," a Shoreman noted, "our local artists would have nothing to paint." One farmer told me, "I haven't got enough money to fix it up and I'm too old and sentimental to tear it down." But in any case, demolition is expensive. J. T. Holland, a former Northampton County supervisor, suggested that there are two reasons for not tearing a building down: there is not enough money, or there is too much. Too much money allows you not to care. Indeed, only members of a truly wealthy society can afford to abandon their dwellings. Many of our empty houses would appear as mansions to people in other parts of the world.

The structures I photographed are forsaken, deserted. No further energies are to be expended upon them, not even the energy required to tear them down. Often a wreck of a building squats in the middle of a field, forcing a farmer to make tortured and elaborate turns when plowing his field. It would be so much easier to burn the house or barn—in a few minutes the land would be cleared. But it isn't so simple. Sometimes the building is owned by many members of a family, and the cost of searching for the legal owners might be very high.

We wonder why buildings are abandoned and not torn down; why do we so seldom see them as eyesores? I seriously doubt that the abandoned trailers, tract houses, and prefabricated structures of the twenty-first century will evoke the same feelings of affection these "old-fashioned" structures do. But for now, architecture continues to have a strong hold over us even after the building no longer serves its purpose. Our attachment surely has something to do with our thoughtful attention to historic change, its patterns, its causes—with a sort of rational nostalgia. "No other artifact," wrote Bernard Herman, "visually marks the passage of historic time, of stability and change, of cultural continuity and flux more than does architecture." But I suspect the reason for our fascination draws more deeply on our feelings of mystery, romance, compassion. We all can be losers in life; finally we all are gone, in a sense abandoned. "There is a certain beauty in poverty, loss, and desolation," wrote Hugh Prather in *Notes to Myself*. "There is a certain strength and grandeur in suffering. . . . Even a dump heap can evoke admiration."

UNREAL ESTATE

Ruins provide the incentive for restoration, and for a return to origins. There has to be (in our new concept of history) an interim of death or rejection before there can be renewal and reform. The old order has to die before there can be a born-again landscape. . . . The old farmhouse has to decay before we can restore it and lead an alternative life style in the country; the landscape has to be plundered and stripped before we can discover it and gentrify it. That is how we reproduce the cosmic scheme and correct history.

JOHN BRINCKERHOFF JACKSON
The Necessity for Ruins and Other Topics, 1980

RUE

NEW CHURCH

JERKVILLE

OYSTER

The wood-frame house has been one of the most prevalent forms of shelter in the United States since the days of the early settlers. As a result, there are houses of various ages in outmoded and deteriorating condition in almost every community across the country. Some are being razed while others are simply abandoned. In either case they must be replaced by a new living unit at a high cost and with the consequent drain on our natural resources. Many of these homes could be rehabilitated at a lower cost than that of new construction and with desirable material savings.

GERALD E. SHERWOOD
New Life for Old Dwellings, 1975

GREENBACKVILLE

14

TEMPERANCEVILLE

PENNYVILLE

CHANCETOWN

PIGGEN

LOCUSTVILLE

WATTSVILLE

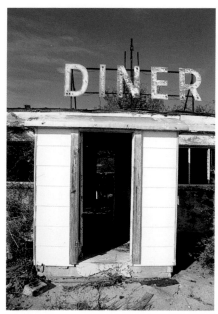

TASLEY

BRIDGETOWN

HALLWOOD

EASTVILLE

NASSAWADOX

NEW CHURCH

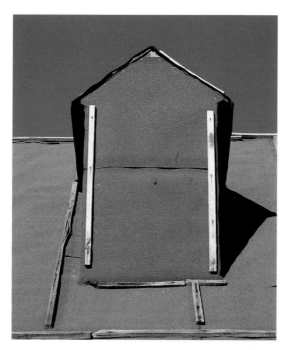

BIRDSNEST

SAVAGEVILLE

A building, however artless, however innocent of conscious speech on the part of the builder, by its very presence cannot help saying something. Even in the plainest esthetic choices of materials, or of proportions, the builder reveals what manner of man he is and what sort of community he is serving.

LEWIS MUMFORD
Art and Technics, 1952

DEEP CREEK

BOBTOWN

The physician can bury his mistakes, but the architect
can only advise his client to plant vines.

Frank Lloyd Wright
An American Architecture, 1955

MODEST TOWN

BLOXOM

FROGSTOOL

Sometimes the progress of man is so rapid that the desert reappears behind him. The woods stoop to give him a passage, and spring up again when he is past. It is not un-common . . . to meet with deserted dwellings in the midst of the wilds; the traveler frequently discovers the vestiges of a log house in the most solitary retreats, which bear witness to the power, and no less to the inconstancy, of man.

ALEXIS DE TOCQUEVILLE

Democracy in America, volume 2, 1838

COBB ISLAND

COBB ISLAND

WALLOPS ISLAND

BOSTON

NELSONIA

KELLER

OLD TROWER

HORNTOWN

LATIMER SIDING

CAPE CHARLES

MACEDONIA

CAPE JUNCTION

WHITESVILLE

Careful analysis may reveal that an old building is literally beyond repair or, more likely, that the costs of reconstruction far exceed those of replacement. In that case, abandoning the project is the only rational choice.

WILLIAM C. SHOPSIN
Restoring Old Buildings for Contemporary Uses, 1986

Born in the Netherlands, but now a full-time resident of Virginia's Eastern Shore, Robert de Gast is a photographer and writer with a lifelong interest in architecture and landscape. He has restored several abandoned houses and spends as much time as he can sailing the waters around the Shore. His previous books include *The Oystermen of the Chesapeake*; *Western Wind, Eastern Shore*; and *The Lighthouses of the Chesapeake*, which is also available from Johns Hopkins.